yours to
Keep!

America's ANIMAL COMEBACKS

American Bison

A Scary Prediction

by William Caper

Consultants:
Rick Wallen, Wildlife Biologist
Bison Ecology and Management Program
Yellowstone National Park

Matt Kales
U.S. Fish and Wildlife Service

BEARPORT
PUBLISHING

New York, New York

Credits

Cover and Title Page, © Sascha Burkard/Shutterstock; 4, © The Granger Collection, New York; 5, © tbkmedia.de/Alamy; 7, © The Granger Collection, New York; 8, © The Granger Collection, New York; 9, © Jim Peaco/Yellowstone National Park Service; 10, © Denver Public Library, Colorado Historical Society, and Denver Art Museum, Call No. Z-89; 11, © Francis G. Mayer/Corbis; 12, © Bettmann/CORBIS; 13, © Burton Historical Collection/Detroit Public Library; 14, © The Granger Collection, New York; 15, © Yellowstone National Park Service; 16, © Smithsonian Institution Archives, Negative No. 2003-19498; 17, © Smithsonian Institution Archives, Negative No. 74-12338; 18, © WCS, Image No. 964638250; 19, © Denise DeMello/WCS, Image No. DD_2501_BX_Zoo_Signage; 20, © Library of Congress, LC-USZ62-102416; 21, ©WCS, Image No. E01EEbz; 22, © Wichita Mountains Wildlife Refuge/U.S. Fish & Wildlife Service; 23, © Wichita Mountains Wildlife Refuge/U.S. Fish & Wildlife Service; 24, © Bryan Henry/Yellowstone National Park Service; 26, © Richard A. Cooke/Corbis; 28, © J. Schimdt/Yellowstone National Park Service; 29T, © J.Giustina/Peter Arnold, Inc.; 29B, © Kenneth Fink/Photo Researchers Inc; 31, © Gregory James Van Raalte/Shutterstock.

Publisher: Kenn Goin
Senior Editor: Lisa Wiseman
Creative Director: Spencer Brinker
Photo Researcher: Beaura Ringrose
Cover Design: Dawn Beard Creative

Library of Congress Cataloging-in-Publication Data

Caper, William.
  American bison : a scary prediction / by William Caper.
     p. cm. — (America's animal comebacks)
  Includes bibliographical references and index.
  ISBN-13: 978-1-59716-504-4 (library binding)
  ISBN-10: 1-59716-504-2 (library binding)
  1. Hornaday, William Temple, 1854–1937—Juvenile literature. 2. American Bison Society—Juvenile literature. 3. American bison—Juvenile literature. I. Title. II. Series.

SF401.A45C37 2007
599.64'30973—dc22

                                   2007010863

For more information, write to Bearport Publishing Company, Inc., 101 Fifth Avenue, Suite 6R, New York, New York 10003. Printed in the United States of America.

10 9 8 7 6 5 4 3 2 1

Contents

A Shocking Prediction

It had been a long day. William Temple Hornaday, a **zoologist**, and his team of workers were in Montana looking for bison. More than three weeks had gone by and they had not seen even one of the large creatures. It was hard for Hornaday to believe that millions of these animals had once roamed the American plains.

William Hornaday was a leader in helping to save American bison.

Only three years later, in 1889, Hornaday made a **prediction** that shocked many people. He said that in ten years wild American bison would be **extinct**. The only ones left would be living in zoos or on ranches.

Something had to be done to save the bison from extinction. Or was it already too late?

Millions of bison once roamed North America.

Bison use their small horns to defend themselves from enemies and to fight for a spot within a **herd**.

Bison Were Here First

There were bison in North America long before people arrived. It's believed that bison **migrated** across a **land bridge** that once joined Asia and Alaska about 35,000 years ago.

By the time people settled in North America, bison were almost everywhere. They were as far south as what is today Mexico. They lived as far east as what is today New York. Most of them, however, lived on the **Great Plains**.

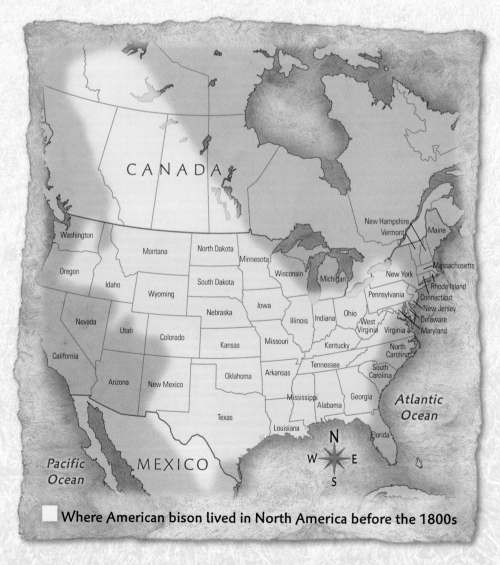

Where American bison lived in North America before the 1800s

Scientists don't know exactly how many bison there were. It's thought, however, that at one time 30 to 60 million lived in North America.

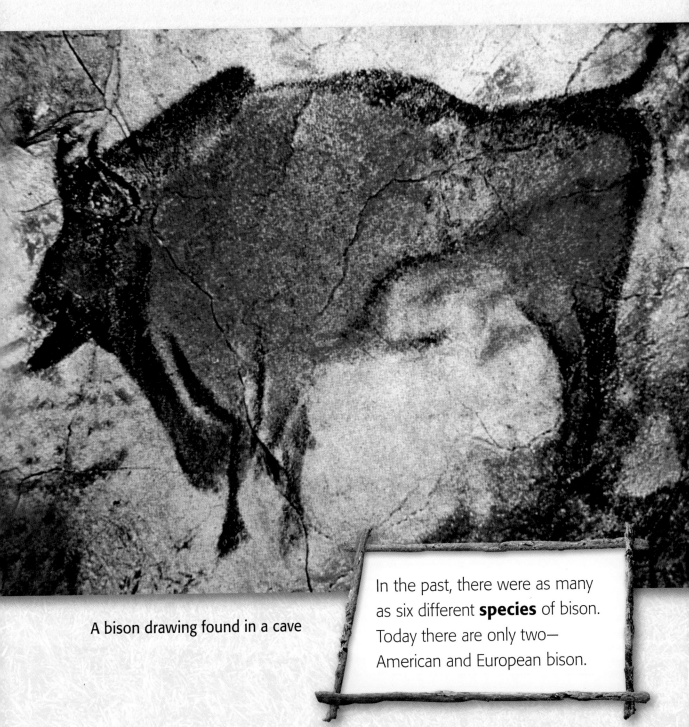

A bison drawing found in a cave

In the past, there were as many as six different **species** of bison. Today there are only two—American and European bison.

Bison and Native Americans

Some Native Americans who settled in North America depended on bison. For thousands of years, they hunted the large animals for food, clothing, and shelter.

The hunters used almost every part of the animal. They ate bison meat. Bison skins, called hides, were used to make clothing, boats, armor, cups, bags, and drumheads. Horns and bones became tools and decorations.

Some Native Americans hunted bison with bows and arrows or with spears.

Some Native Americans **worshipped** bison as part of their religion. They used the animals' skulls and other parts during ceremonies.

A Lakota leader and his son perform a bison ceremony.

The Lakota are a Native American group. Their word for bison is *tatanka* (ta-TAHN-ka).

The Slaughter Begins

Early European explorers came to North America about 500 years ago. They found so many bison that they could not count them. One explorer said the country looked like a "black robe" because so many animals covered the land.

A large bison herd

Like Native Americans, Europeans hunted bison. They hunted with guns, which allowed them to kill many animals quickly. They used the hides to make robes and ate bison tongues for a tasty treat.

As settlers moved west, more and more bison were killed. By the 1830s, almost all the bison were gone in the eastern half of the United States.

Guns made it possible for hunters to kill millions of bison quickly.

Though bison are heavy, they are fast runners. Some can run up to 40 miles per hour (64 kph).

The Killing Increases

In the 1860s, things got even worse for bison. Workers started building train tracks across the country for the Union Pacific and other railroads. The railroads hired hunters like William F. Cody to provide bison meat for the workers to eat. In 17 months, this famous hunter killed more than 4,000 animals.

William F. Cody was also called "Buffalo Bill."

Bison hides were also in great demand. To some people, killing the animals was a way to get rich fast. They could sell the hides for a lot of money.

As the killing continued, the bodies of dead bison filled the plains. People gathered the bones, ground them up, and sent them to other cities. They were then used as **fertilizer**.

In the 1800s, people could sell ground up bison bones for $5 per ton (metric ton).

Almost Extinct

By 1870, only two large groups of bison remained in the Great Plains—the southern and northern herds. Within five years, the southern herd was destroyed. Ten years later, the northern herd was gone, too.

Bison did not run away when members of their herd were shot. This allowed hunters to kill many of them at one time.

By 1889, less than 1,000 wild bison were left in the United States. That was the year that William Hornaday made his scary predication.

Killing bison became a **sport**. Hunters shot them from the windows or roofs of trains.

The Man Who Saved the Bison

William Temple Hornaday worked at the United States National Museum in Washington, D.C. In 1886, Hornaday set out for Montana with a group of workers. They hoped to find lots of bison to bring back to the museum. During their eight-week trip, the team found only a few bison. There were once millions of bison in North America. Hornaday knew these large animals were in trouble.

Hornaday probably brought this baby bison named Sandy back from his trip to Montana.

To make people aware of the bison problem, Hornaday published a book called *The **Extermination** of the American Bison* in 1889. In it, he told the history of the huge creature's terrible treatment by people. Unless this treatment changed quickly, Hornaday predicted, the wild American bison would soon no longer exist.

Schoolchildren look at the first bison at the National Zoo in Washington, D.C.

The bison Hornaday found in Montana were put in the National Zoo in Washington, D.C. They were among the zoo's first animals.

Bison at the Bronx Zoo

Unfortunately, Hornaday's prediction did not scare enough people. Hunters continued to kill these animals. By 1893, there were only about 300 wild bison left.

Hornaday brought bison to the Bronx Zoo.

Hornaday, however, was determined to save these creatures. In 1896, he became the first director of the Bronx Zoo in New York. Working at the zoo allowed Hornaday the chance to do more for bison. In 1899, he started a bison herd with animals that were **donated** to the zoo. This herd grew. By 1913, there were about 42 bison living at the zoo.

Today, the Bronx Zoo has grown to include thousands of animal exhibits.

Hornaday worked at the Bronx Zoo for 30 years. He helped to make it one of the best and largest zoos in the world.

The American Bison Society

William Hornaday continued to help the bison. On December 8, 1905, he established the American Bison Society. This was one of the country's first **conservation** groups. It worked to protect bison.

Hornaday in his office at the Bronx Zoo

Today, the American Bison Society is part of the Wildlife Conservation Society. This group saves wild animals and lands around the world. Its headquarters is at the Bronx Zoo in New York.

Hornaday was president of the American Bison society. Theodore Roosevelt, the nation's President at the time, was also a member of the group. He asked Congress to create wildlife **preserves** for bison. Soon the country's first bison preserve opened in Oklahoma in 1907. The government also set up other protected **habitats** in Montana, South Dakota, and Nebraska.

President Roosevelt (center) helped Hornaday save the bison.

A Big Year for Bison

Finally, the nation was making an effort to save the bison by providing safe homes for them. The American Bison Society also hoped to rebuild their **population**. To do so, in 1907, the Bronx Zoo sent about 15 bison to the preserve in Oklahoma. There, the animals could grow into a new, bigger herd. Within six years, the herd grew to 37 animals!

Bison from the Bronx Zoo arrived in Oklahoma by train. They traveled the rest of the way to their new home in wagons.

Canada was also helping save the bison. In 1906, Canada's government bought a herd of bison from an American ranch. A year later, the herd was sent to Elk Island National Park, a new Canadian preserve.

Many of today's bison in the western United States are **descendents** of the Bronx Zoo bison that were sent to Oklahoma in 1907.

Bison and their calves roam the plains at the Wichita Mountains National Wildlife Refuge in Oklahoma.

Where the Bison Roam

Today there are parks with bison in North Dakota, South Dakota, and several other states. The largest group of **free-ranging** bison in the United States has about 4,000 animals. These animals live in Yellowstone National Park. There are also bison herds in some Canadian parks.

Yellowstone National Park began to **restore** their bison herd in 1902. They added 21 animals to the group of 23 that were already living in the park.

Yellowstone National Park was the first national park in America. It stretches into parts of Wyoming, Idaho, and Montana.

Not everyone is happy about the free roaming bison, however. Some animals can carry **diseases** that might harm cattle. Ranchers, **biologists**, and others are working to stop contact between wild bison and cattle.

Where American bison live in North America today

Yellowstone National Park

A Success Story

It is **estimated** that there are now 200,000 to 450,000 bison in North America. About 20,000 live on preserves. Thanks to the hard work of William Hornaday and others, many think of bison as the United States' first **environmental** success story. Once almost extinct, these animals are no longer in danger.

A bison herd in South Dakota

For some people, saving the bison has meant saving a symbol of the American West. For others, it has meant even more. It shows that human effort can bring a species back from near extinction. It also shows that if people can help the American bison, other animals can be saved as well.

Today, South Dakota has more bison herds than any other state.

Bison Facts

Population: **North American population before the 1800s:** about 30–60 million
North American population today: about 200,000–450,000 on ranches; about 20,000 on preserves and in parks

Weight	Length	Height	Fur Color
Male: 1,600–2,000 pounds (726–907 kg)	Male: 10–12.5 feet (3–4 m)	Male: 5.5–6 feet (1.7–1.8 m)	brown
Female: 800–1,200 pounds (363–544 kg)	Female: 7 feet (2 m)	Female: 5 feet (1.5 m)	

Food	Life Span	Habitat
grass; also some other small plants and shrubs	about 20–30 years on ranches; Yellowstone bison live about 12–14 years	United States and Canada

Other Bovidae in Danger

The American bison is one kind of animal in the bovidae (BOH-vi-day) family making a comeback by increasing its numbers. Other members of the bovidae family are also trying to make a comeback.

Cuvier's Gazelle

- There are fewer than 2,500 Cuvier's (KYOO-vee-ayz) gazelles in the world.

- They live in the African countries of Algeria, Morocco, and Tunisia.

- Today, loss of habitat is the main threat to these animals.

- Fourteen African countries are working together to protect them and other endangered animals.

- Cuvier's gazelles born in zoos have been released in the wild in Tunisia.

Western Giant Eland

- There are fewer than 2,500 western giant elands in the world.

- The western giant eland is a type of antelope. It is one of the largest antelopes in Africa.

- The western giant eland is in danger because of hunting and habitat destruction.

- The African countries of Guinea and Mali have laws protecting the western giant eland.

Glossary

biologists (bye-OL-uh-jists) scientists who study plants and animals

conservation (*kon*-sur-VAY-shuhn) the protection of wildlife and nature

decendents (di-SEND-uhnts) people or animals that come from a family that lived earlier in time

diseases (duh-ZEE-zez) illnesses

donated (DOH-nate-id) gave something as a gift

environmental (en-*vye*-ruhn-MEN-tuhl) having to do with the land, air, and sea

estimated (ESS-ti-*mate*-id) guessed the amount of something

extermination (ek-*stur*-muh-NAY-shuhn) the killing off of large numbers of animals

extinct (ek-STINGKT) when a kind of plant or animal has died out; no more of its kind is living anywhere in the world

fertilizer (FUR-tuh-*lize*-uhr) a substance used to help make soil richer so crops will grow

free-ranging (FREE-*raynj*-ing) allowing animals to move about freely

Great Plains (GRAYT PLANEZ) the grasslands in North America that cover much of the central United States and parts of Canada and Mexico

habitats (HAB-uh-*tats*) places in nature where plants or animals normally live

herd (HURD) a large group of animals

land bridge (LAND BRIJ) a narrow piece of land that connects larger pieces of land

migrated (MYE-grate-id) moved from one place to another

population (*pop*-yuh-LAY-shuhn) animals or people living in an area

prediction (pri-DIK-shuhn) a statement about what is going to happen in the future

preserves (pri-ZURVZ) protected areas of land set aside for animals or plants

restore (ri-STOR) to bring back; to establish again

species (SPEE-sheez) groups that animals are divided into according to similar characteristics; members of the same species can have offspring together

sport (SPORT) something done for fun or adventure

worshipped (WUR-shipd) showed love and devotion to something or someone

zoologist (zoh-OL-uh-jist) a person who studies animals

Bibliography

www.americanwest.com/critters/buffindx.htm

www.northern.edu/natsource/MAMMALS/Bison1.htm

www.nps.gov/archive/thro/tr_buffs.htm

Read More

Berman, Ruth. *American Bison.* Minneapolis, MN: Carolrhoda Books (1992).

Brodsky, Beverly. *Buffalo.* New York: Marshall Cavendish (2003).

Robbins, Ken. *Thunder on the Plains: The Story of the American Buffalo.* New York: Atheneum Books for Young Readers (2001).

Winner, Cherie. *Bison.* Minnetonka, MN: NorthWord Press (2001).

Learn More Online

To learn more about bison, visit
www.bearportpublishing.com/AnimalComebacks

Index

About the Author

William Caper has written books about history, science, film, and many other topics. He lives in San Francisco with his wife, Erin, and their dog, Face.